A Child's First Library of Learning

Ecology

TIME-LIFE BOOKS • ALEXANDRIA, VIRGINIA

Contents

Are All Forests the Same?

ANSWER There are many kinds of forests all over the world. The trees that grow in them are very different. The kind of forest that grows in a place depends on the climate. The temperature may be warm or cold. The weather may change from one season to the next. Or there may be a lot of rain.

■ Forests in hot places

Tropical rain forests grow in places where it is hot all year and there is a lot of rain. Many of the different kinds of trees in a tropical rain forest have broad leaves, which they keep all year long.

■ Forests in mild places

Temperate forests grow in places where the weather changes from season to season. Here, many trees lose their leaves in the fall. They grow new ones in the spring.

■ Forests in cold places

Evergreen forests grow in places that have long, cold winters and very short summers. Most of the trees have needlelike leaves that stay green all year.

● **To the Parent**

Tropical rain forests cover large parts of South America, Africa, and Southeast Asia. Temperate forests are common in Europe, East Asia, and much of the United States. Evergreen forests are often found in northern Europe, Russia, and Canada. In many parts of the world there are mixed forests, which include features of more than one type.

5

❓ What Is a Tropical Rain Forest?

World rain forests

Tropical rain forests cover many parts of
Southeast Asia, the Amazon River Basin in
South America, parts of Mexico and Central
America, and the Congo River Basin in Africa.

ANSWER A tropical rain forest is a place filled with life. All year long there is hot weather and plenty of rain. In a tropical rain forest trees grow and grow. These dense forests are home to many plants and animals. About half of all the kinds of animals living on earth can be found in rain forests.

The top branches of rain forest trees come together to form a dense canopy that shuts out much of the sunlight. Most rain-forest animals live in this canopy. The forest floor is warm, damp, and dark. Fallen plants decay quickly here, releasing lots of nutrients that are rapidly absorbed by trees and other plants.

●To the Parent

Tropical rain forests are a vital part of the earth's ecosystem. The extensive rain forest surrounding the Amazon basin in South America produces one-fourth of the world's oxygen and contains two-thirds of all the river water on the planet. Most rain forests are tropical, but there are some in temperate regions, such as the one found in the state of Washington.

? Why Do Animals Need Forests?

ANSWER Many animals live in a forest. The plants are a rich source of food such as fruits, nuts, berries, and leaves. Because there are lots of places to hide, the forest can be a safe place to make a home. Many animals live in its trees. They have babies and raise their young while living there.

Summer

▶ In warm summer weather, forest trees provide shade and food. In the winter, they are a place to escape the cold and to rest.

▼ The large trees and thick bushes in a forest help animals hide from their enemies.

Winter

■ Forests are full of food

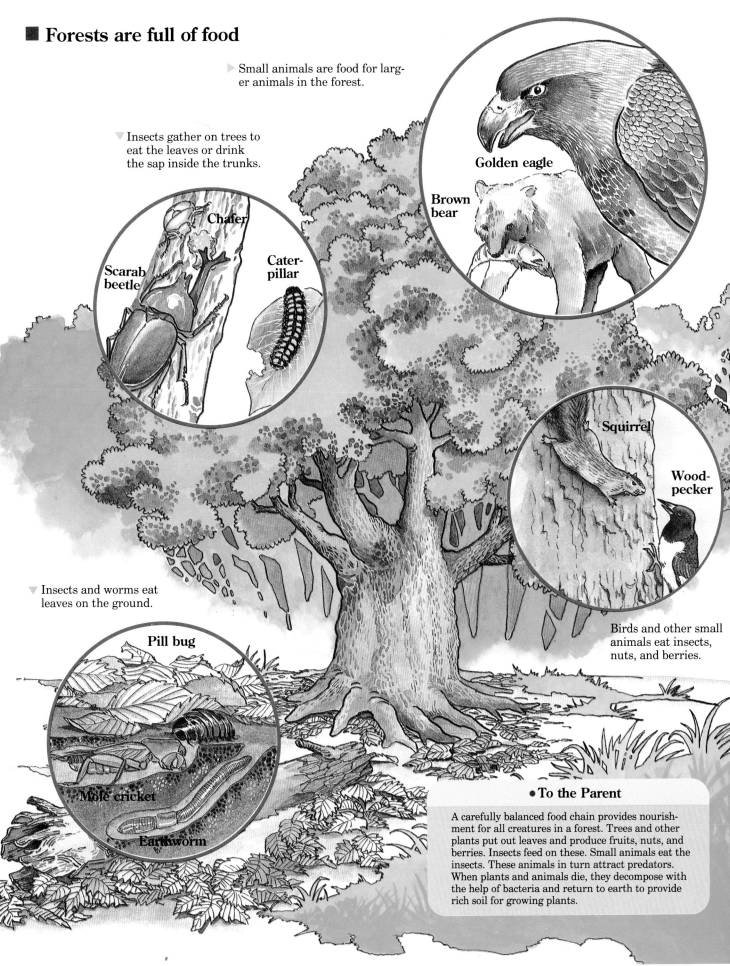

▶ Small animals are food for larger animals in the forest.

▼ Insects gather on trees to eat the leaves or drink the sap inside the trunks.

Chafer

Scarab beetle

Cater-pillar

Golden eagle

Brown bear

Squirrel

Wood-pecker

▼ Insects and worms eat leaves on the ground.

Pill bug

Mole cricket

Earthworm

Birds and other small animals eat insects, nuts, and berries.

● To the Parent

A carefully balanced food chain provides nourishment for all creatures in a forest. Trees and other plants put out leaves and produce fruits, nuts, and berries. Insects feed on these. Small animals eat the insects. These animals in turn attract predators. When plants and animals die, they decompose with the help of bacteria and return to earth to provide rich soil for growing plants.

Why Are Forests Disappearing?

ANSWER More people are alive now than ever before. They need places to grow food and places to live. As people spread out, they cut down forests to make room. They also use the trees in the forest to make paper, furniture, firewood, and lumber for building. If too many trees are cut down, the earth's forests will disappear.

■ More and more people

1800 →

■ Firewood

For some people wood is a main source of energy. Trees are cut down and used for cooking and heating.

■ Cleared for farming

Tropical rain forests are cut down and burned. The land then becomes a field for planting crops.

The number of people on earth is growing fast. For every one person alive in 1800, there will be six people living on earth in the year 2000.

2000

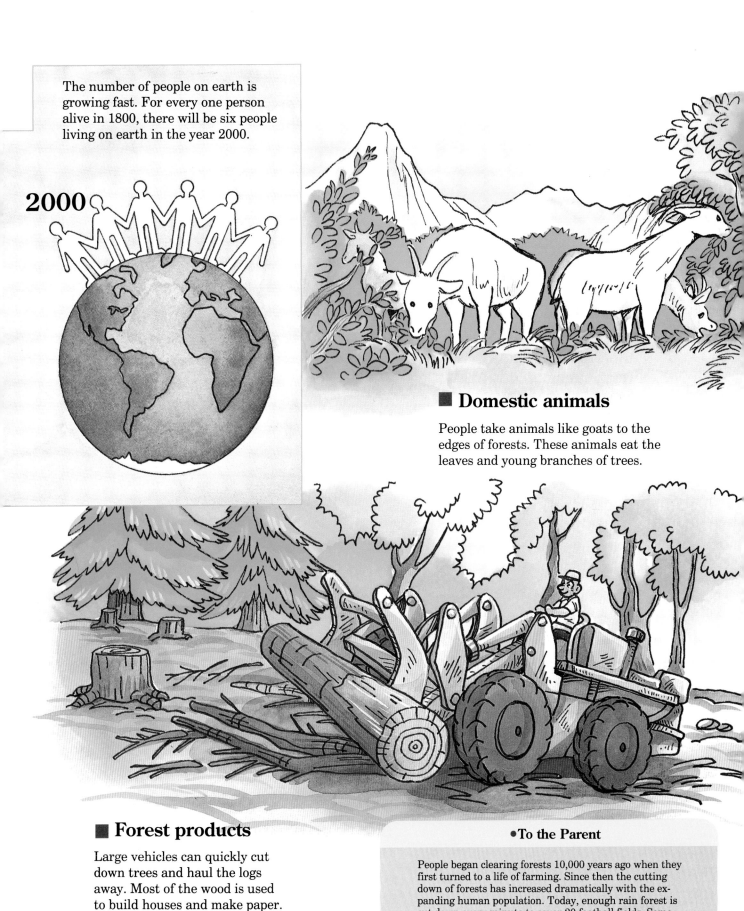

■ Domestic animals

People take animals like goats to the edges of forests. These animals eat the leaves and young branches of trees.

■ Forest products

Large vehicles can quickly cut down trees and haul the logs away. Most of the wood is used to build houses and make paper.

●**To the Parent**

People began clearing forests 10,000 years ago when they first turned to a life of farming. Since then the cutting down of forests has increased dramatically with the expanding human population. Today, enough rain forest is cut down every minute to cover 20 football fields. Some countries with temperate forests replant trees to help maintain this precious resource.

? Why Is Acid Rain So Dangerous?

ANSWER We think of rainwater as clean and pure. Sometimes that is not the case. In cities, air pollution from cars and factories can send harmful gases into the sky. The wind then carries the polluted air away from the city. When rain mixes with the gases and falls to the ground, it harms trees. Within a few years, this polluted rain also causes plant and animal life in lakes to die.

Acid rain fell on this forest. It soaked into the soil, damaging trees and their roots.

Some acid rain can be as strong as the vinegar in salad dressing.

To the Parent

Acid rain originates with the oxides of nitrogen and sulfur emitted by factories, power plants, and cars. When these gases combine with rain, it develops a strong sulfuric acid content. When acid rain enters the soil, it harms the root systems of trees. It also disrupts the food chain in lakes and rivers. Pollution controls and the spraying of lime to neutralize the acid are the best methods for combating this problem.

Why Are Green Plants Important to People and Other Animals?

ANSWER

The leaves of a green plant make food for the plant. They take a gas called carbon dioxide from the air we breathe out. They mix this gas with water and sunlight to make the food they need. When they are finished, the leaves release a gas called oxygen into the air. People and animals need oxygen to live.

▲ Plants in dense rain forests produce a lot of oxygen. Rain forests along the Amazon River in South America make about one-fourth of the world's oxygen.

Oxygen

■ **Forests clean the air we breathe**

Carbon dioxide

■ Plants help the soil

The roots of trees and plants reach down into the soil and help hold it together. The ground is then able to store water.

▶ If the trees are cut down from a mountainside, there is nothing to hold the soil in place. A little rain can wash away a lot of soil. A heavy rainfall can cause a flood.

◀ Without trees, the rich topsoil cannot store rainwater. Over time, the topsoil washes away.

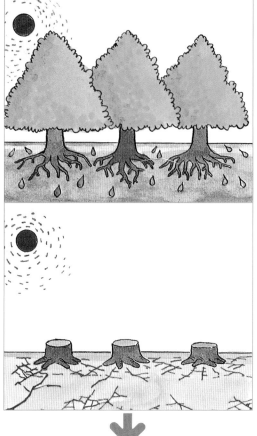

▲ Water flowing down the side of a mountain without trees flooded this village.

▲ Very few plants will grow on land that cannot store water. This area eventually became a wasteland.

● To the Parent

Green plants perform many functions vital to other living things. Photosynthesis cleans the air of carbon dioxide and produces oxygen as a by-product. The root systems of trees and plants hold together soil and prevent erosion. Deforestation can lead to mud slides and avalanches on mountains and floods at lower altitudes. It can cause topsoil erosion, which turns fertile areas into barren wastelands.

What Can We Do to Save Trees?

(ANSWER) We can do many things to save trees. We can set aside forests where trees will never be cut down. We can plant new trees. We can also use the products that come from trees wisely. We can help protect trees from pests and diseases that kill them.

■ Take care of forests

Be careful when you camp or hike in a park or forest. Put garbage in a trash can or take it home with you. Don't break off branches or carve anything in a tree trunk. If you light a campfire, be sure it is out before you leave.

Many important things are made from trees. Paper and pencils are two examples. Use these things when you need them, but do not waste them. And recycle paper whenever you can.

What Is Being Done Now to Protect Trees?

Many people now understand that it is important to protect trees. In some forests, they plant new trees to replace the ones that are cut down. They are also setting aside national parks or preserves where trees cannot be cut down or harmed in any way. They are trying to find ways of keeping trees healthy by stopping the spread of pests and diseases. And they are recycling things made from trees.

▲ Spraying trees with chemicals helps protect them from the damaging effects of such pests as gypsy moths.

▲ When a tree is cut down, a new one can be planted to replace it.

▲ In parks and preserves no one is allowed to harm trees or animals.

Recycling helps, too. If old newspapers are used to make paper, fewer trees need to be cut down.

● To the Parent

The loss of forestland has raised concerns around the world. Children may become worried when reading about the alarming rate of deforestation. Taking an active role in conservation may help children feel they are doing something to help solve this worldwide problem. They can be taught to reuse and recycle products such as paper. They can also be taught to respect plant life, whether in a national park or in their own backyard.

Where in the Ocean Do Fish Live?

(ANSWER) The seas and oceans of the world are large and deep. Most fish live in the shallower parts where sunlight reaches. Here there are plants and smaller fish to eat. A few fish live where it is too deep for sunlight.

Flying fish

Portuguese man-of-war

Bluefin tuna

Bonito

500 ft.

■ Where the fish live

Mackerel shark

■ Continental shelf

Where land and ocean meet there is an underwater ledge, called the continental shelf. It reaches out to the deeper parts of the ocean. Many fish live in the water over the continental shelf.

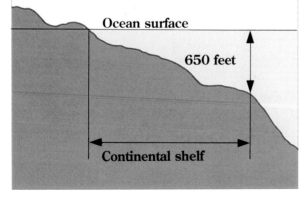

Ocean surface

650 feet

Continental shelf

3,250 ft.

Lizardfish

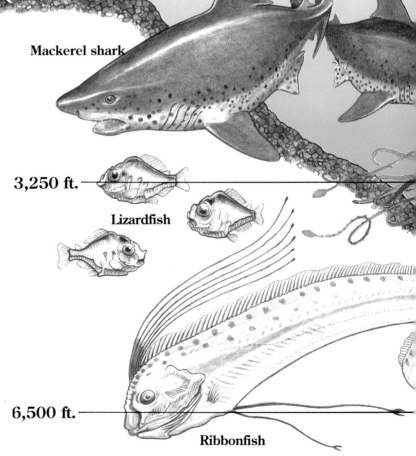

6,500 ft.

Ribbonfish

18

■ How about seaweed?

Most kinds of seaweed need sunlight to live, so they grow near the surface of the water. Many grow 30 to 60 feet below the surface, where there is still lots of light. Dark red seaweed does not need as much sunlight and is found in deeper water.

■ On the ocean floor

Special submarines have explored the deeper parts of the ocean, where sunlight does not reach. They have discovered that some ocean creatures live here, too.

Sunfish

Basking shark

Squid

Eel

•To the Parent

In the ocean, as on land, sunlight is a key ingredient for life. In the layers near the surface, microscopic plants called phytoplankton use sunlight, dissolved minerals, and carbon dioxide to make food. These plants are the foundation of the ocean food chain. Since food is abundant near the surface, most fish live in these upper layers, at depths of 650 feet or less.

❓ Why Are Whales Disappearing?

■ Some of the largest and rarest whales

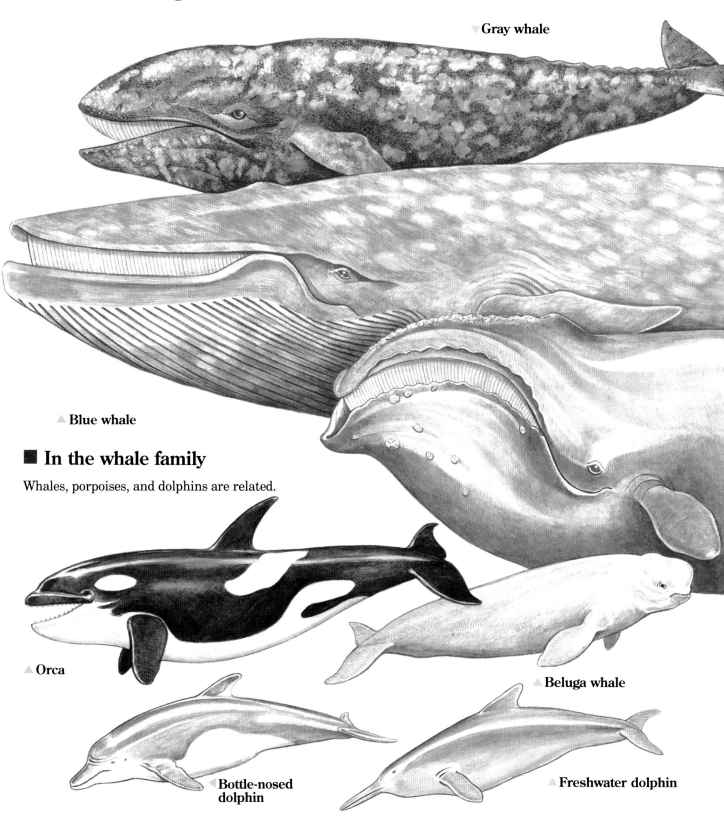

▼Gray whale

▲Blue whale

■ In the whale family

Whales, porpoises, and dolphins are related.

▲Orca

▲Beluga whale

◀Bottle-nosed
dolphin

▲Freshwater dolphin

(ANSWER) Whales are the largest animals that have ever lived. Since ancient times people have hunted whales for their meat and their oil. Whales are big but cannot defend themselves. Because too many were hunted, they began to disappear. Today most countries have stopped hunting whales.

■ Vanishing whales

Blue whale

Southern right whale

Some whale populations are very small. Today there are about 4,000 blue whales and fewer than 2,000 right whales. That may sound like a lot, but compared with the population long ago it is quite small.

▲ Southern right whale

Sperm whale

■ Two kinds of whales

Right and blue whales have bony plates, or baleen, that filter food from the water. Other whales have teeth. The sperm whale is the largest of these.

●To the Parent

The modern whaling industry has brought whales to the edge of extinction. In 1946 the International Whaling Commission was set up to place limits on the amount of whaling. In 1985 the commission banned commercial whaling. In spite of the ban, the governments of some countries still allow their citizens to hunt whales.

 What Causes Ocean Pollution?

■ Pollution reaches the sea

ANSWER Ocean water is polluted in different ways. Sometimes things are dumped or spilled right into it. Waste and chemicals are also washed into the ocean from homes, factories, and farms.

▼ The water people use in their homes gets dirty. Much of this wastewater leaves their houses through sewer pipes that carry it away. Many factories get rid of their waste in a similar way. Most of this wastewater ends up in rivers, lakes, and oceans. If it is not cleaned first, it can pollute the water.

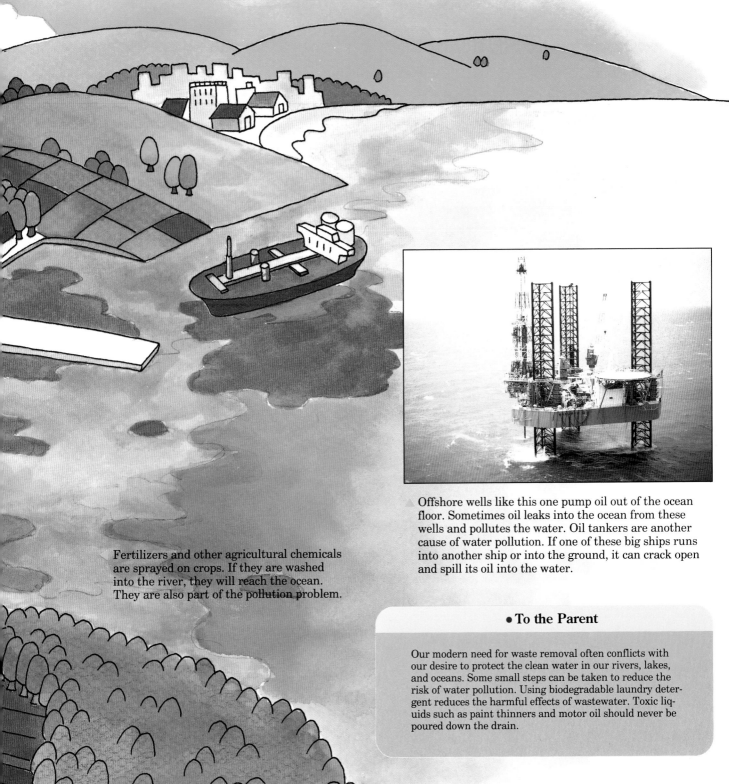

Offshore wells like this one pump oil out of the ocean floor. Sometimes oil leaks into the ocean from these wells and pollutes the water. Oil tankers are another cause of water pollution. If one of these big ships runs into another ship or into the ground, it can crack open and spill its oil into the water.

Fertilizers and other agricultural chemicals are sprayed on crops. If they are washed into the river, they will reach the ocean. They are also part of the pollution problem.

● **To the Parent**

Our modern need for waste removal often conflicts with our desire to protect the clean water in our rivers, lakes, and oceans. Some small steps can be taken to reduce the risk of water pollution. Using biodegradable laundry detergent reduces the harmful effects of wastewater. Toxic liquids such as paint thinners and motor oil should never be poured down the drain.

Why Are Oil Spills in the Ocean Such a Big Problem?

(ANSWER) Oil is carried across the ocean in the largest ships ever made. They are called supertankers. If a tanker has an accident, millions of barrels of oil can pour into the water. Big oil spills cause problems for seabirds, fish, and other animals.

■ A fence for oil

Before a tanker unloads oil, a floating oil fence is set up. If oil spills, the fence keeps it near the tanker. Then a specially built ship can clean up most of it. Fences are also used to collect some oil after spills in the ocean.

■ Cleaning up a spill

When a tanker has an accident, much of the spilled oil floats away. If it is not gathered quickly, it spreads out. If it reaches the shore, the oil must be cleaned up by hand.

■ Spraying a spill

Another way to clean up spills is to spray the oil with a chemical that turns it into a solid. That makes it easier to lift the oil out of the water. Sometimes oil-eating bacteria are used to help remove the spill.

● To the Parent

Oil spills from supertankers are huge ecological disasters. The 1989 spill in Alaska dumped 11 million barrels of oil into Prince William Sound. A spill of this size far exceeds the self-cleansing capabilities of the ocean. After a spill, the oil slick spreads out. As much as half of the oil evaporates. Much of what is left forms sticky clumps called mousse. Sunlight and oil-eating organisms dissolve some of the mousse. The rest forms tar balls that stay in the environment.

How Does Oil Harm Ocean Animals?

ANSWER The ocean is home to many plants and animals. When oil gets in the water, it changes their home. Some animals die because they can't breathe or are poisoned. Others cannot find enough food to eat. Marine animals with feathers or fur cannot live when they are covered with oil.

■ **A spreading oil slick**

■ **Harming the food chain**

When an oil slick covers the surface of the water, it stops air from getting to the water below. That creates problems for many animals in the ocean's food chain.

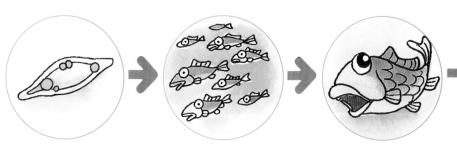

▲ Tiny plants and animals called plankton that live near the water's surface disappear.

▲ Small fish that feed on plankton and big fish that eat the small fish become fewer and fewer.

❓ How Do Seabirds Get the Oil off Their Feathers?

Birds normally use their beaks to clean off their feathers. This is called preening. If they swallow the oil while preening, they will die. That is why people must catch oily birds quickly and wash them.

A seabird's feathers are designed for life in the ocean. When the feathers are covered with oil, a bird may no longer be able to fly or stay warm.

▲ Animals that eat fish get scarcer and scarcer because there is not enough food for them.

● **To the Parent**

A large oil spill presents many problems for sea creatures. It disrupts the food chain by killing some animals and contaminating others. Birds are among the most visible victims of most spills. Their oil-soaked feathers lose their insulating and waterproofing properties, leaving the birds unprotected against the elements. After the oil spill in Alaska's Prince William Sound, 300,000 seabirds died. In most cases, people must capture birds, clean their feathers, and release them if they are to survive.

Why Are Wetlands So Important?

ANSWER Wetlands are places where water and land meet. The ground is often soft and muddy, so people cannot get around very well. But for many animals it is the perfect home. There is lots for them to eat, and they find shelter in the tall plants that grow there. Wetlands are also important for the environment. They absorb water from heavy rains so there is not as much flooding, and they help clean pollutants out of the water.

Some wetlands are found at the edges of lakes and along the banks of rivers.

■ **An African wetland**

Hammerhead

Hippopotamus

In a wetland, grasses and other plants cover the soft ground. The feet of the wild animals that live there are flat and wide or can be spread wide. This lets them walk without sinking into the mud.

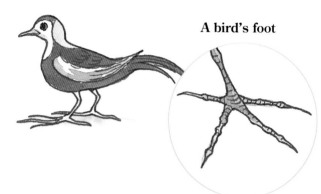

A bird's foot

A deer's foot

Kingfisher

Spoonbill

When a swamp starts to dry up, a lungfish makes a hole in the mud and waits there for rain.

Catfish

Lungfish

●To the Parent

Once thought of as little more than mosquito-infested wastelands, marshes, swamps, and other wetlands were often drained to make the land available for human use. Today wetlands are recognized as valuable habitats. Two-thirds of commercially harvested fish and shellfish spawn or mature in coastal wetlands. Wetlands also act as nature's water-treatment plants. Their soil and plants absorb pollutants from water that drains into them.

❓ Are Lakes and Ponds the Same?

ANSWER Most water ends up in the ocean, but it collects in other places too. A lake is a large body of water. Lakes are often filled by rivers and streams flowing into them. Most have fresh water, but some are salty like the ocean. Ponds are similar to lakes, but they are smaller and much shallower. Ponds are rarely more than 15 feet deep. The deepest lake is over 5,000 feet deep.

■ Lakes, marshes, and ponds

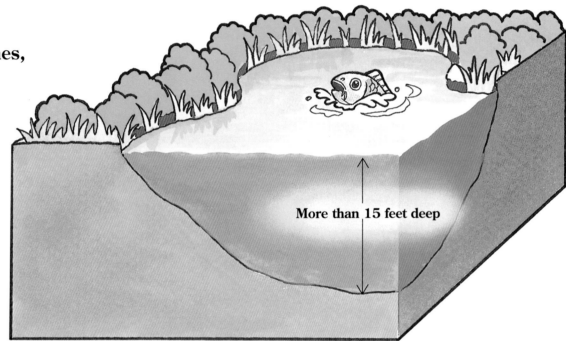

Large, deep lakes

Lakes are more than 15 feet deep. Sunlight does not reach all the way down where the lake is deepest. In this part of the lake, no plants grow on the bottom.

More than 15 feet deep

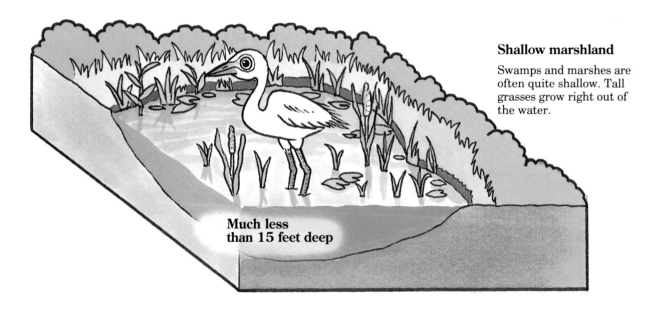

Shallow marshland

Swamps and marshes are often quite shallow. Tall grasses grow right out of the water.

Much less than 15 feet deep

Ponds are smaller

Sunlight reaches down into a small pond.
Even in the middle where it is deepest,
plants may be growing beneath the surface.

Less than 15 feet deep

■ Making lakes

Where a dam stops a river from flowing, a lake forms behind it. Sometimes
these man-made lakes are used as
reservoirs. They provide water for
drinking, farming, and industry.

❓ What Happens When a Lake Gets Old?

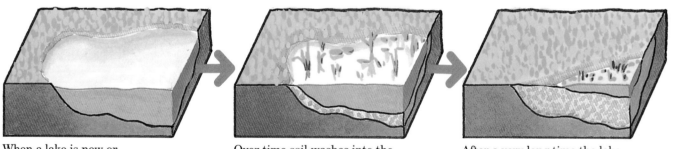

When a lake is new or
very young, its water is
deep and clear.

Over time soil washes into the
lake. Plants move in around
the edges.

After a very long time the lake
turns into marshland.

The three pictures above show how a lake may very slowly
change into a marsh. A lake is filled with water from rivers and streams. Some soil is washed into the lake, too.
Leaves are blown there by the wind and settle on the lake
bottom. Trees and other plants begin to grow in the newly
formed soil around the edges. Over a very long time the lake
gets shallower. Eventually it can dry up completely and become just like the land around it.

❓ How Do Fish Live in River Water That Is Moving Very Fast?

(ANSWER) Only fish that are strong swimmers can live in the parts of a river where the current is strong. They must swim against the flow of the water just to stay in the same spot. Some fish stay near the river bottom where the water moves slower.

▲ Char

■ Fish face upstream

In fast-moving water, fish face the direction the water is coming from. They catch food that is carried downstream by the current. Fast-moving water is also rich in oxygen. Fish that face upstream can breathe easily.

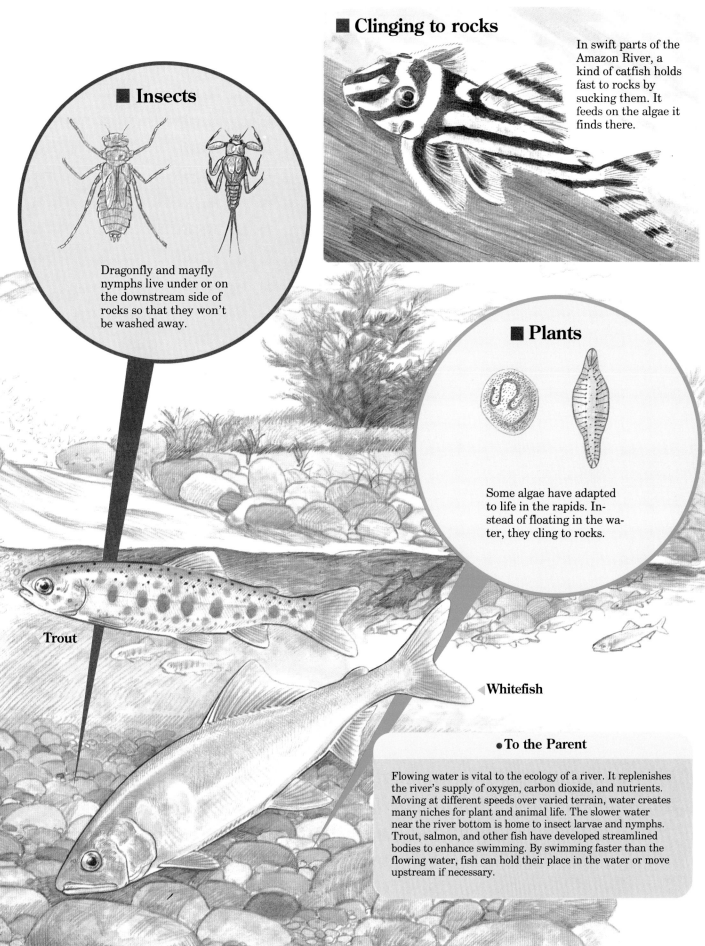

■ Clinging to rocks

In swift parts of the Amazon River, a kind of catfish holds fast to rocks by sucking them. It feeds on the algae it finds there.

■ Insects

Dragonfly and mayfly nymphs live under or on the downstream side of rocks so that they won't be washed away.

■ Plants

Some algae have adapted to life in the rapids. Instead of floating in the water, they cling to rocks.

Trout

Whitefish

● To the Parent

Flowing water is vital to the ecology of a river. It replenishes the river's supply of oxygen, carbon dioxide, and nutrients. Moving at different speeds over varied terrain, water creates many niches for plant and animal life. The slower water near the river bottom is home to insect larvae and nymphs. Trout, salmon, and other fish have developed streamlined bodies to enhance swimming. By swimming faster than the flowing water, fish can hold their place in the water or move upstream if necessary.

Why Are Rivers and Lakes Important?

■ **Using rivers and lakes**

Dams along rivers make reservoirs that hold fresh water. In some places, water flowing from dams is used to produce electricity.

In many countries rivers are used like roads. They move people and products from one place to another.

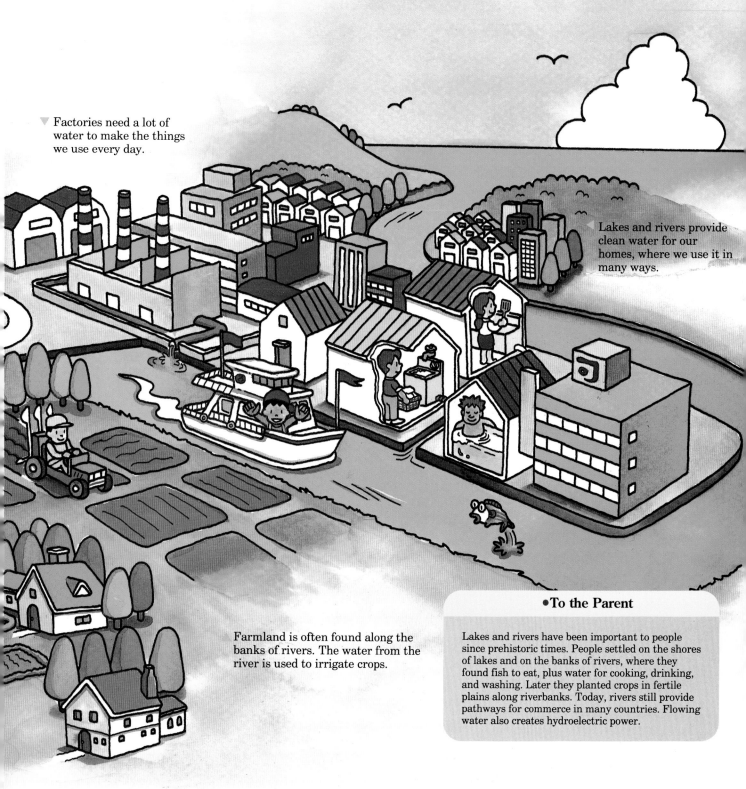

ANSWER People have always lived near rivers and lakes. They provide water to drink and food to eat. Rivers are important for other reasons, too. These bodies of water are roadways that help people to travel from one place to another. Some rivers are also important sources of energy.

▼ Factories need a lot of water to make the things we use every day.

Lakes and rivers provide clean water for our homes, where we use it in many ways.

Farmland is often found along the banks of rivers. The water from the river is used to irrigate crops.

•To the Parent

Lakes and rivers have been important to people since prehistoric times. People settled on the shores of lakes and on the banks of rivers, where they found fish to eat, plus water for cooking, drinking, and washing. Later they planted crops in fertile plains along riverbanks. Today, rivers still provide pathways for commerce in many countries. Flowing water also creates hydroelectric power.

How Do We Get the Water We Need?

(ANSWER) People use a lot of clean water. They get it in many ways. Some of it comes from lakes and rivers. Water is also pumped out of the ground. In some countries, rainwater is collected. In others, salt is removed from seawater so people can drink it.

Collecting rainwater

In places where pure water on the ground is scarce, rainwater is sometimes collected. It is usually cleaned before drinking.

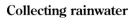

From rivers and lakes

Water pumped from rivers and lakes is often treated. A water-treatment plant cleans the water, making it safe for drinking and other purposes.

Using seawater

Much of our planet's water collects in its oceans. Because it is salty, people cannot drink it. At a desalinization plant the salt is removed, making water for drinking and other uses.

■ Sources of water

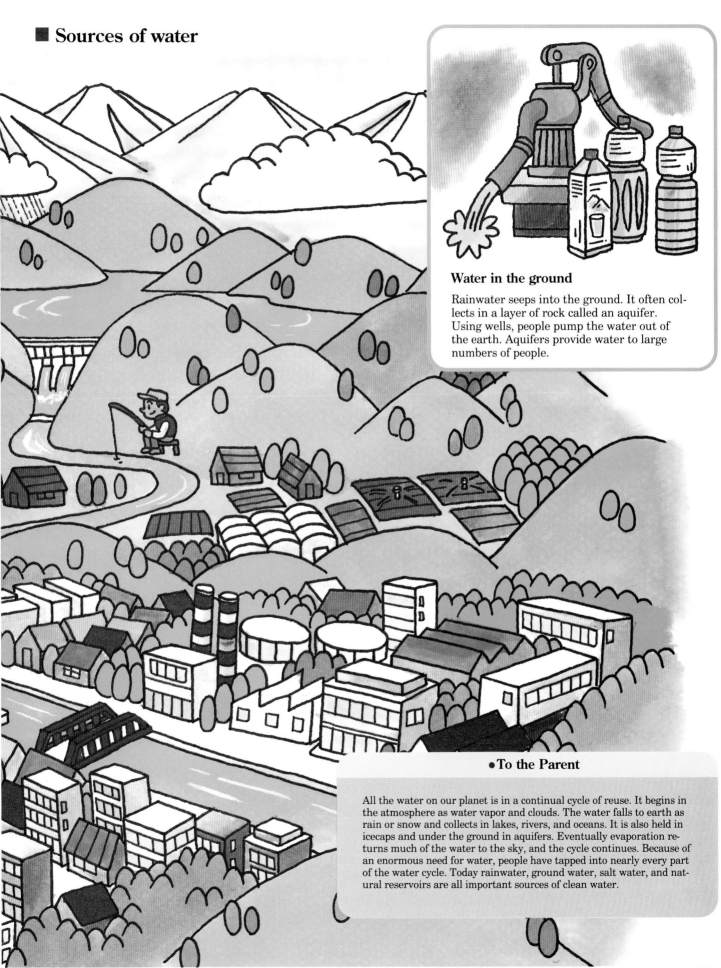

Water in the ground

Rainwater seeps into the ground. It often collects in a layer of rock called an aquifer. Using wells, people pump the water out of the earth. Aquifers provide water to large numbers of people.

Why Are Rivers and Lakes Polluted?

(ANSWER) On farms and in cities and towns people use a lot of water. Fertilizers and other chemicals from farms are washed into our rivers. So is dirty water from factories. In our homes we rinse water down the drain and flush it down the toilet. Much of this water ends up in our lakes and rivers.

On the farm

Fertilizers and other chemicals put on crops can pollute ground water, rivers, and lakes.

Water from factories

Factories use a lot of water. If this water is dumped into rivers and streams without first being cleaned, it can cause pollution.

Clean water used in factories, farming, and our daily lives gets filthy.

Water we use at home

The water we use in our homes is polluted by detergents, grease, and human waste.

How Is Dirty Water Cleaned?

Water that has become polluted can be cleaned at sewage-treatment plants. First much of the solid material is removed from the water. Then other steps are taken to clean the water so it is safe enough to put back into rivers.

◀ A sewage-treatment plant.

▲ Some detergents today are made so they will not pollute water. Their labels say that they contain no phosphates and are biodegradable.

Some materials can cause water pollution even in small amounts. To get rid of the contamination caused by a single table-spoon of oil, you must spread it out in 15 bathtubs of water.

● To the Parent

Wastewater from homes and factories is often cleaned in sewage-treatment plants. In a mechanical stage, the water is filtered through screens and then put into tanks where some suspended solids settle out. This process, called primary treatment, reduces gross pollutants in the water. In secondary treatment, biological methods such as aeration are used to further reduce pollutants. In some cases there is one more treatment stage to make the water safe for return to lakes and rivers and eventual human use.

Why Are Some Deserts Spreading?

ANSWER Deserts are the world's driest places. Where a desert ends, tall grasses, trees, and other plants may grow. Sometimes people clear the land next to deserts for farming. They also raise animals that graze on the plants. When people are not careful, the desert spreads over this land.

▲ Africa's Sahara, the world's largest hot desert, is still growing. It is spreading out at its borders.

■ How deserts spread

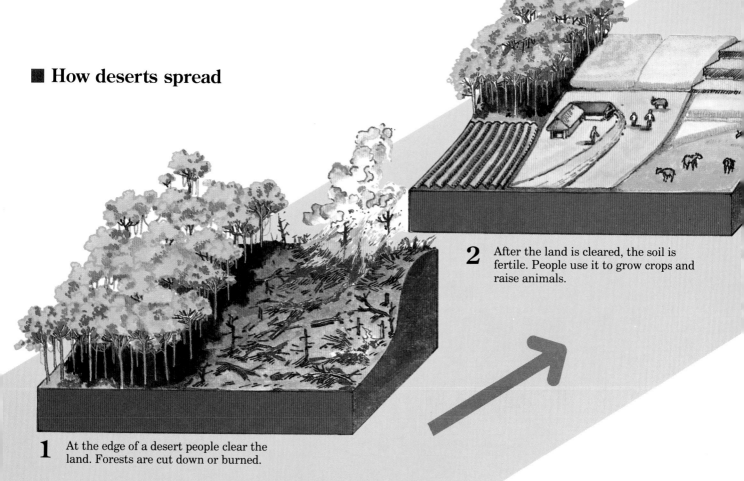

1 At the edge of a desert people clear the land. Forests are cut down or burned.

2 After the land is cleared, the soil is fertile. People use it to grow crops and raise animals.

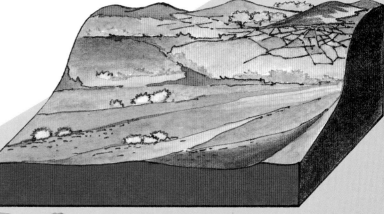

4 The people move away. With poor soil and little water, plants cannot return to the land. It has become part of the desert.

3 Over time the soil becomes less fertile. As the land becomes bare, there are no plants to hold the soil together and trap water. The land becomes drier.

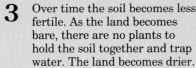

■ The changing desert

Some deserts grow and change because of the action of nature. Strong, dry winds sweep across deserts. With little to stop it, the wind gradually breaks down rocks. Wind also builds sand dunes, which move slowly with it. The wind can carry dunes into the land next to the desert, making the desert bigger.

● To the Parent

Deserts and near-deserts cover about one-third of the earth's land surface. Desertification claims 80,000 square miles every year. A growing human population has resulted in overplanting of crops, cutting of forests, and overgrazing of livestock on lands that border deserts. The depleted soil cannot stop the desert's encroachment.

How Can Animals Live in the Desert Where It Is So Hot?

(ANSWER) When the sun is out, the hottest place in a desert is on the ground. It is much cooler under the ground. This is where many desert animals go to escape the scorching heat of the desert day.

A camel's long legs keep its body in the cooler air above the hot desert ground. Its hump is mostly fat, which it uses for energy when food is scarce.

■ Some desert animals

The sand lizard has hoods that keep the sand out of its eyes and nostrils.

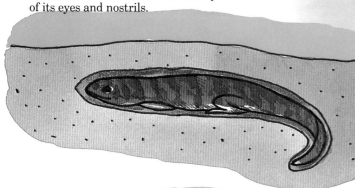

The jerboa spends the day sleeping in its burrow underground. During the cool night, it comes out to find seeds and insects for food.

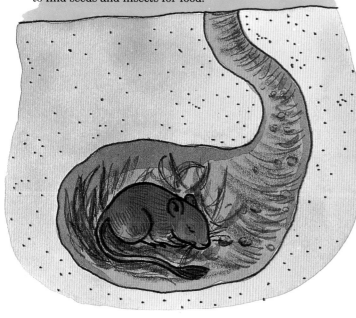

The spadefoot toad digs into the ground. It spends as long as 9 months buried in dried mud waiting for desert rain to fall.

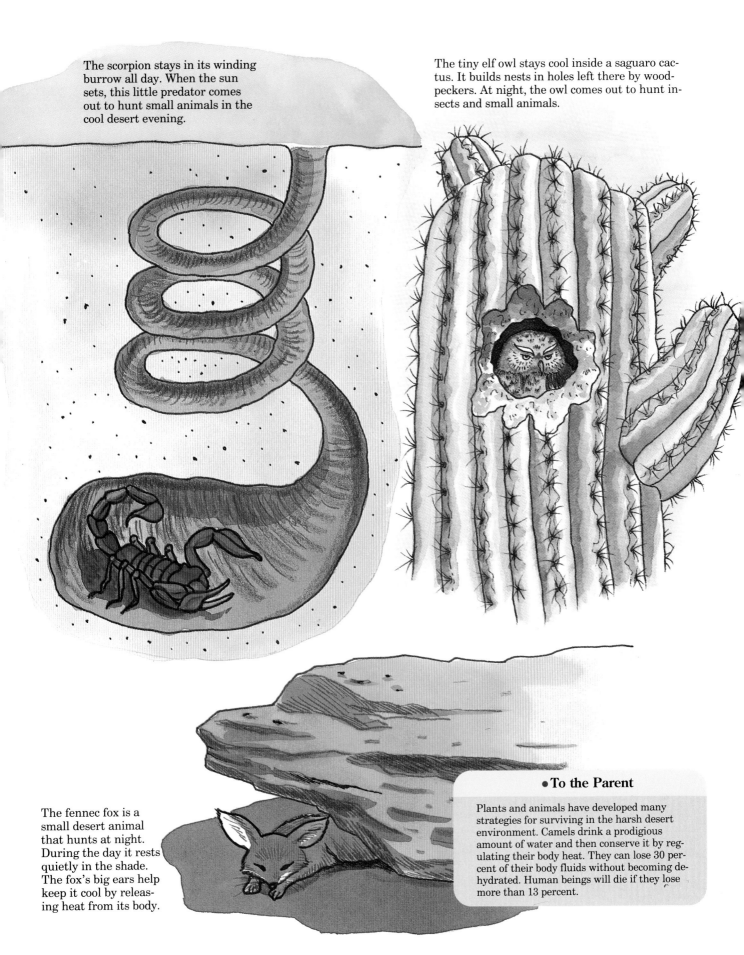

The scorpion stays in its winding burrow all day. When the sun sets, this little predator comes out to hunt small animals in the cool desert evening.

The tiny elf owl stays cool inside a saguaro cactus. It builds nests in holes left there by woodpeckers. At night, the owl comes out to hunt insects and small animals.

The fennec fox is a small desert animal that hunts at night. During the day it rests quietly in the shade. The fox's big ears help keep it cool by releasing heat from its body.

● **To the Parent**

Plants and animals have developed many strategies for surviving in the harsh desert environment. Camels drink a prodigious amount of water and then conserve it by regulating their body heat. They can lose 30 percent of their body fluids without becoming dehydrated. Human beings will die if they lose more than 13 percent.

❓ Does a Desert Have Any Water?

ANSWER Even though deserts are the earth's driest places, a little rain or snow falls in many of them. Some deserts also have pools of water called oases. They are places where water comes out of the ground.

▲ Plants burst into life around a desert oasis. Animals may journey long distances to reach the water.

■ How an oasis forms

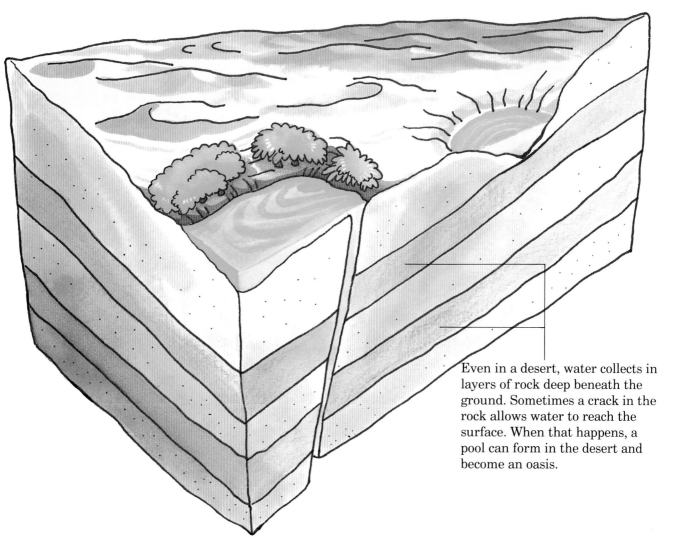

Even in a desert, water collects in layers of rock deep beneath the ground. Sometimes a crack in the rock allows water to reach the surface. When that happens, a pool can form in the desert and become an oasis.

■ How plants store water

▶ When it rains, a cactus soaks up water like a sponge. The plant stores the water and uses it slowly during dry days.

Water drops

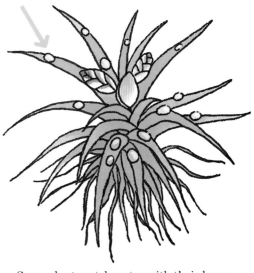

▲ Some plants catch water with their leaves. When the weather cools, drops of dew form on the leaves. The drops roll down to where the leaves meet the stem and are taken in by the plant.

■ Rain in the desert

At times, it rains very hard in the desert. Plants store as much water as they can. Animals come out and use the water, too.

● To the Parent

A great deal of water is held in the ground below a desert. In some places the underground strata crack and separate. An oasis forms where water courses through the crack to the surface. To reach water stored beneath the desert surface, some plants, like the mesquite, have roots that descend 20 to 60 feet.

Why Don't Grasslands Have Trees?

(ANSWER) Grasslands are open plains. There is more rain than in a desert, but still these are dry places. That is why only a few kinds of grasses and low trees can grow in a grassland.

A herd of wildebeest roams a grassland in Africa called a savanna.

■ Different grasslands

Grasslands are found on many continents. They usually form near the center, away from moist ocean breezes. Grasslands have different names from place to place.

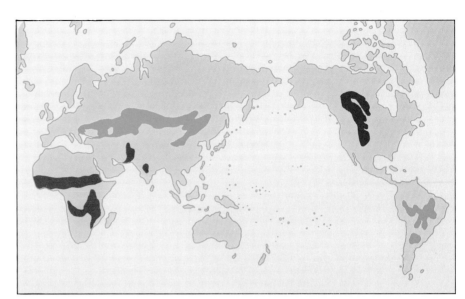

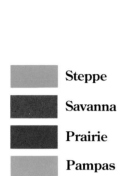
Steppe

Savanna

Prairie

Pampas

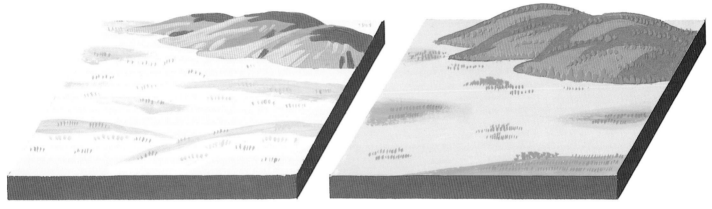

▲ Steppe

▲ Pampas

▲ Savanna

The steppes are grasslands that stretch from Europe to Asia. On the North American prairie, the grasses are taller in the east and shorter out west. African savannas have tall grass and some flat-topped trees. On South America's pampas, most grasses are medium in height. On all grasslands the height of the grass depends on the rainfall.

▲ Prairie

●To the Parent

On most grasslands, the climate is too wet for the development of deserts and too dry for the growth of forests. Grasslands in tropical regions receive more rain than other grasslands, but usually at only one time of year. The long dry season prevents the growth of forests. Huge areas such as the American prairie and the Eurasian steppe have zones in which different varieties of grasses grow depending on temperature, rainfall, and soil fertility.

47

Why Do Grasses Grow So Well in Grassland Soil?

ANSWER Grasses grow well because grassland soil is usually very fertile. In many countries, grasslands have been turned into farms where crops like wheat, oats, and barley grow.

▼ Grassland soil

■ Different soils

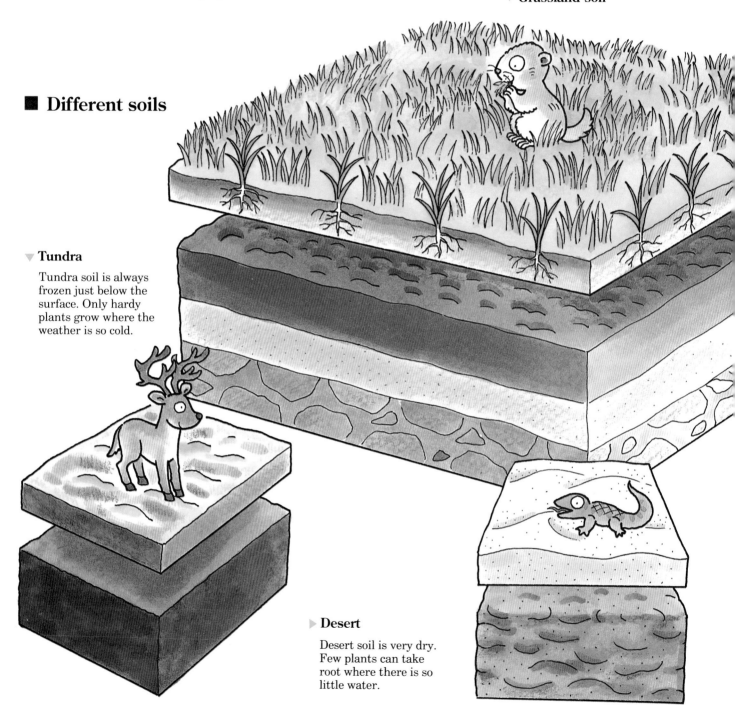

▼ Tundra

Tundra soil is always frozen just below the surface. Only hardy plants grow where the weather is so cold.

▶ Desert

Desert soil is very dry. Few plants can take root where there is so little water.

■ Soils of the world

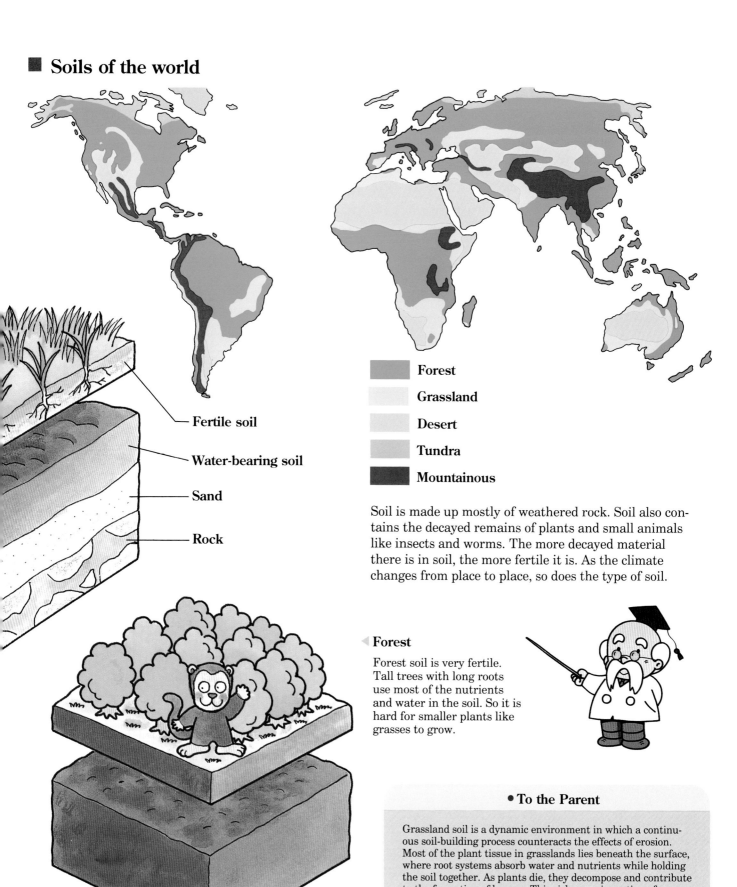

Fertile soil

Water-bearing soil

Sand

Rock

Forest

Grassland

Desert

Tundra

Mountainous

Soil is made up mostly of weathered rock. Soil also contains the decayed remains of plants and small animals like insects and worms. The more decayed material there is in soil, the more fertile it is. As the climate changes from place to place, so does the type of soil.

◀ **Forest**

Forest soil is very fertile. Tall trees with long roots use most of the nutrients and water in the soil. So it is hard for smaller plants like grasses to grow.

● To the Parent

Grassland soil is a dynamic environment in which a continuous soil-building process counteracts the effects of erosion. Most of the plant tissue in grasslands lies beneath the surface, where root systems absorb water and nutrients while holding the soil together. As plants die, they decompose and contribute to the formation of humus. This rich organic portion of grassland soil is very absorbent. It increases the soil's ability to hold water while providing nitrogen and other elements vital to plant growth.

What Animals Live on Grasslands?

ANSWER Many animals live on grasslands, including the world's largest land animals. For plant eaters, the grasses and other plants that grow there provide plenty of food. The African savanna, in particular, is home to herds of large plant eaters. The herds, in turn, provide food for meat eaters.

■ **Plant eaters**

▶ Giraffe

▼ Ostrich

Impala

▲ Buffalo

▶ Rhinoceros

▲ Elephant

50

■ Meat eaters

Large herds of plant eaters attract hunters such as lions. Other predators feed on smaller animals, such as mice, that live in the tall grasses.

▷ **Lion**

▷ **Rattlesnake**

◁ **Peregrine falcon**

▲ **Hyena**

■ Insect eaters

Armadillo

▲ **Anteater**

Grasslands are home to many insects, including grasshoppers, termites, and ants. They are food for animals like anteaters and armadillos.

● **To the Parent**

Grasslands are home to animals of all sizes. Large herbivores, such as zebras, antelopes, and giraffes, live there. So do lions and other carnivores that hunt plant eaters. Small animals, such as prairie dogs, mice, and insects, also thrive. Animal life is vital to the grassland ecosystem. For example, when anteaters and armadillos dig for food, their sharp claws aerate the soil.

51

Why Do We Spray Our Farm Crops with Chemicals?

(ANSWER) The crops we grow are favorite foods for many insects. Sometimes fields are sprayed with chemicals called pesticides. This kills the insect pests that damage crops but can cause problems for larger animals, including people. That is why we must use these chemicals carefully.

■ How pesticides get inside animals

▲ Helicopters are one way pesticides are sprayed.

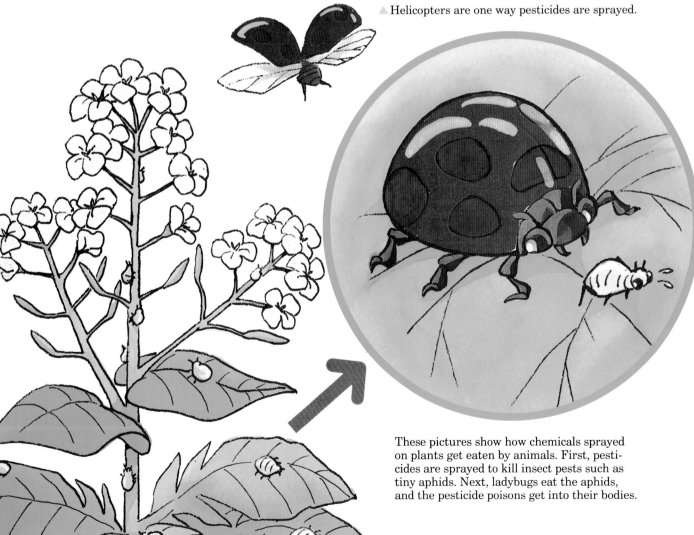

These pictures show how chemicals sprayed on plants get eaten by animals. First, pesticides are sprayed to kill insect pests such as tiny aphids. Next, ladybugs eat the aphids, and the pesticide poisons get into their bodies.

How pesticides stop working

The three drawings below show why some pesticides stop working. At first the chemicals kill most of these flies. But a few *(the ones colored red)* resist the poison. Their children can also resist the poison. As time passes, more and more flies survive. Soon the pesticide stops being effective, and it can no longer be used.

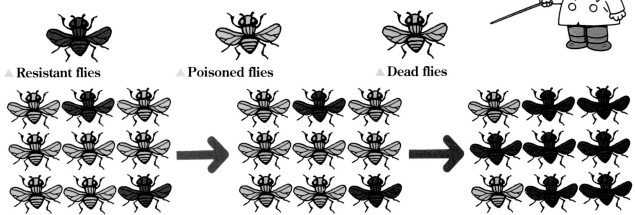

▲ **Resistant flies**　　▲ **Poisoned flies**　　▲ **Dead flies**

1. Flies are sprayed with a pesticide.

2. Many flies die, but a few resist the poison.

3. After a while many flies survive the poison.

Small birds feed on the ladybugs. The pesticides in the insects are now in the birds. Then predators like hawks and falcons eat the birds. The poisonous pesticides build up in the birds' bodies and do great harm.

● **To the Parent**

The use of pesticides to improve crop yields became widespread in the 1950s. Only in recent years have people come to understand the danger of pesticides. Many chemicals, such as DDT, do not break down in nature. As a result of the process called biological accumulation, pesticides build up in greater amounts as they move up the food chain. Traces of pesticides have been found in Antarctic penguins, illustrating the far-reaching nature of the problem.

? Can People Grow Healthy Crops without Poisonous Chemicals?

(ANSWER) All kinds of plants grow without being sprayed with chemicals. Nature has ways of keeping plants healthy and protecting them from some of the insects that would like to eat them. By copying nature's methods, people can often grow crops without using chemicals.

■ Natural fertilizers

When plant and animal matter rots in the soil, it helps make the soil fertile. Straw and other kinds of plants and manure from animals can be spread over crops as fertilizer. In this way, no harmful chemicals enter the soil.

Plowing the earth helps make it more fertile. The plow digs into the soil and mixes the dirt with air, which makes it easier for plants to grow. Turning the soil also provides room for helpful animals like earthworms. Earthworms are nature's plows. When they tunnel through the soil, they mix up the soil and let air in.

■ Getting rid of pests

Unwanted weeds rob crops of space and nutrients. These plant pests can often be removed without using chemicals. Sometimes they can be pulled out by hand. People also cover the ground around healthy plants with shredded bark to keep the sunlight away from weeds so they won't grow at all.

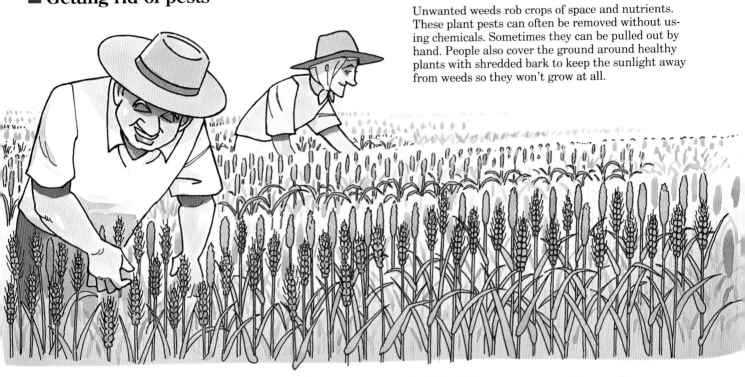

Sometimes people rely on helpful insects to get rid of ones that are pests. Farmers use ladybugs to gobble up harmful aphids before they can destroy crops.

Growing food without harmful chemicals helps us in many ways. It keeps chemicals from washing into rivers and causing water pollution. It protects animal life and helps make the food we eat safe.

What Is the Tundra?

■ Life on the tundra

Arctic fox

▲ Damselfly

Snowy owl

▲ Club moss

Twinflower

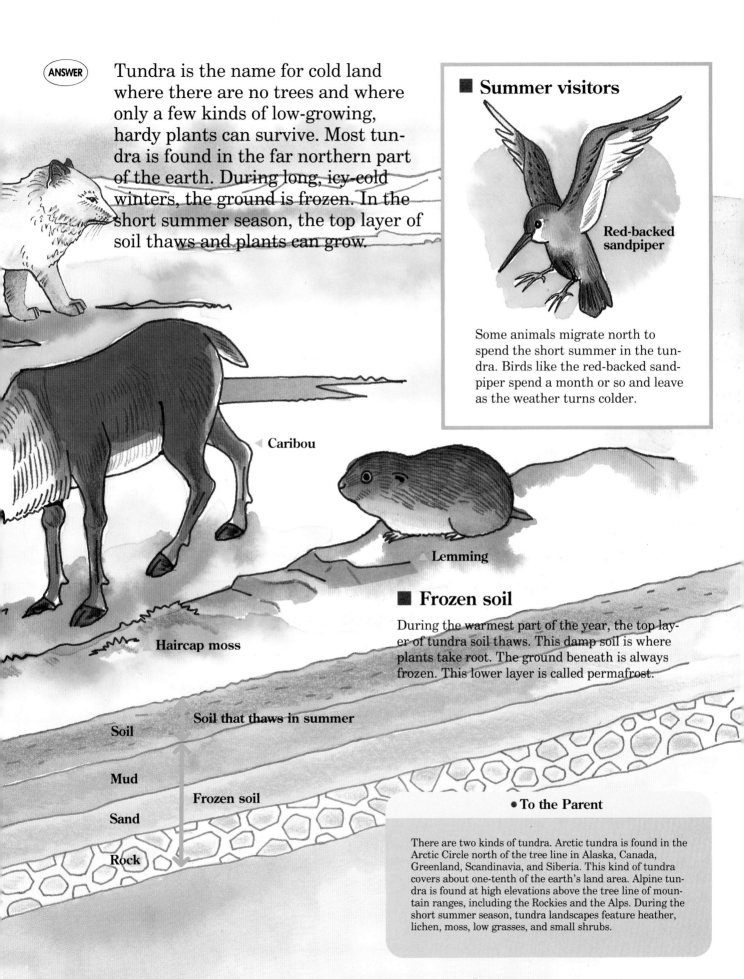

ANSWER Tundra is the name for cold land where there are no trees and where only a few kinds of low-growing, hardy plants can survive. Most tundra is found in the far northern part of the earth. During long, icy-cold winters, the ground is frozen. In the short summer season, the top layer of soil thaws and plants can grow.

Caribou

Lemming

Haircap moss

■ Summer visitors

Red-backed sandpiper

Some animals migrate north to spend the short summer in the tundra. Birds like the red-backed sandpiper spend a month or so and leave as the weather turns colder.

■ Frozen soil

During the warmest part of the year, the top layer of tundra soil thaws. This damp soil is where plants take root. The ground beneath is always frozen. This lower layer is called permafrost.

Soil that thaws in summer

Soil

Mud

Frozen soil

Sand

Rock

● To the Parent

There are two kinds of tundra. Arctic tundra is found in the Arctic Circle north of the tree line in Alaska, Canada, Greenland, Scandinavia, and Siberia. This kind of tundra covers about one-tenth of the earth's land area. Alpine tundra is found at high elevations above the tree line of mountain ranges, including the Rockies and the Alps. During the short summer season, tundra landscapes feature heather, lichen, moss, low grasses, and small shrubs.

57

? Why Is the Arctic Treeless?

ANSWER The area around the North Pole is water covered by ice, so nothing grows there. A bit farther south, the Arctic land is tundra. Trees have little time to grow in the short summer season. Also, their roots cannot take hold in the layers of frozen ground.

The Arctic region of the earth has a harsh climate. It is very cold most of the year, there is little rain, and there are often strong winds. People and animals have found ways to live there, but trees can't survive.

Arctic ice

Water

Land

Besides the harsh climate, trees face another problem in the Arctic. There is very little sunlight. At the North Pole night lasts six months. Trees need lots of light to make food.

During the winter tiny plants cling to the ground to escape the worst of the cold. Tall trees would not be protected from the freezing winds.

What about Antarctica?

Antarctica covers the southern tip of our planet. Antarctica is the coldest place on earth. Most of the land is covered with thick ice all year long. To make survival even more difficult, this continent is a huge desert where little rain or snow falls. The few plants that live there survive using melted ice for water. For the most part only simple plants such as moss and lichens are found on Antarctica. They grow on rocks during the short summer season when the sun shines all day and most of the night.

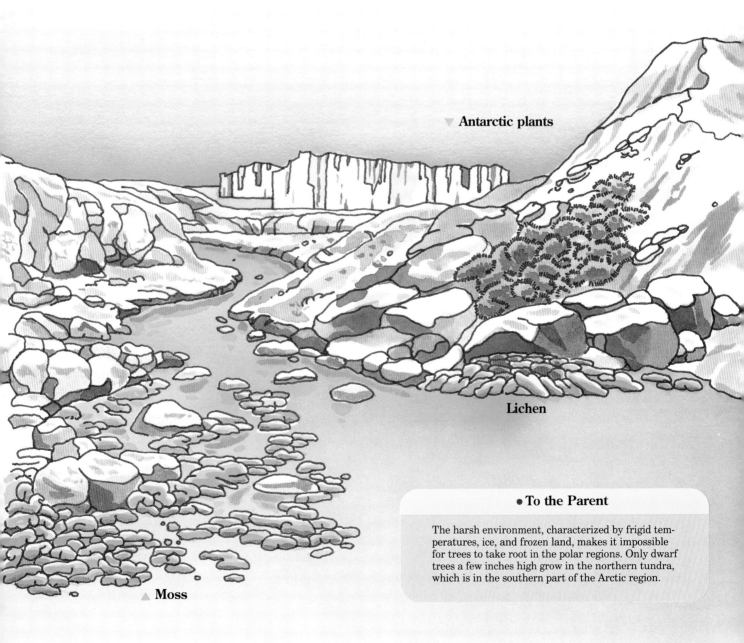

▼ Antarctic plants

Lichen

▲ Moss

● **To the Parent**

The harsh environment, characterized by frigid temperatures, ice, and frozen land, makes it impossible for trees to take root in the polar regions. Only dwarf trees a few inches high grow in the northern tundra, which is in the southern part of the Arctic region.

? How Do Animals Live through the Cold Arctic Winter?

ANSWER When winter comes, many animals leave the Arctic. The small animals that stay burrow into the snow and make warm nests. Large animals have thick fur and a layer of fat that keep them warm.

■ Winter survivors

The polar bear traps air in its thick fur coat. This air is heated by its warm body. Beneath the bear's skin, a layer of fat provides added warmth.

In the fall, female polar bears dig dens in the snow. During the winter they give birth inside. The mothers feed their young and keep them warm until spring.

■ Reindeer leave

During the summer reindeer graze on tundra plants. When winter comes, their food supply is buried under snow. So the reindeer move south in search of food. When summer returns, they go north again to give birth and nurse their young.

▲ Walruses and seals can survive the harsh Arctic winters and frigid waters because they are kept warm by a thick layer of fat, called blubber, just under their skin.

● To the Parent

Arctic animals that do not migrate are equipped to withstand severe Arctic winters. They are well insulated by thick coats of fur or feathers plus layers of fat beneath the skin. Animals that do not hibernate face a second problem—finding food. Large animals like seals and polar bears feed on fish in unfrozen waters. Smaller animals tunnel under the snow where seeds and plants are buried.

? How Do Animals of the Arctic Protect Themselves?

ANSWER The ice-covered Arctic can be a dangerous place for animals. There are no trees or other big plants to hide behind if enemies are near. Many animals use their white color to hide. Other animals use clever tricks to help them survive.

▲ Newborn harbor seals are white as snow.

■ Safe in the snow

Adult harbor seals dive into the sea when danger is near. Seal pups cannot do this. Their white fur is their only protection. Many Arctic animals are white. This lets them blend into the snowy landscape to hide from enemies or, if they are hunters, to surprise prey.

Muskoxen are hunted by wolves. When the oxen sense danger, the herd stands in a circle. Their horns point out in every direction. The little ones stay in the center of the circle where they are safe.

Seals live both on land and in the ocean. When they are attacked on land by polar bears, they dive into the water to get away. When they are attacked in the ocean by killer whales, they climb onto the land to escape.

● **To the Parent**

Many Arctic animals rely on camouflage for protection. The short-tailed weasel, or ermine, is covered with brown fur in summer. In winter it molts and replaces this coat with a snow-white pelt. Arctic hares and foxes also change color. Snowy owls have white feathers. Polar bears and other hunters use camouflage to stalk their prey.

How Can There Be Pollution in the Arctic?

ANSWER No place is completely safe from pollution. The wind carries dirty air to the Arctic. Water pollution arrives on ocean currents. Animals with pesticides in their bodies bring harmful chemicals, too.

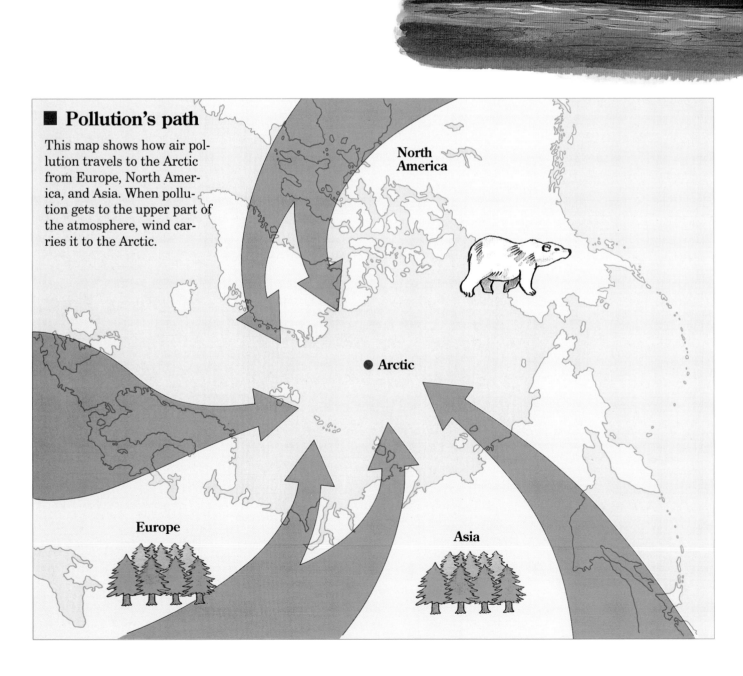

■ Pollution's path

This map shows how air pollution travels to the Arctic from Europe, North America, and Asia. When pollution gets to the upper part of the atmosphere, wind carries it to the Arctic.

North America

● Arctic

Europe

Asia

◼ Nuclear radiation

Sometimes accidents spread pollution. In 1986 an explosion took place in a nuclear power plant at Chernobyl. This city in the Ukraine was once part of the Soviet Union. The disaster sent huge amounts of nuclear radiation into the air. Winds carried the radiation across northern Europe and far into the Arctic.

◼ Leaking oil fields

Huge amounts of oil lie below the seafloor in the Arctic. Oil companies drill into the floor to pump the oil out. If the oil spills or leaks, it can pollute the water.

◼ Nuclear-powered submarines

Nuclear-powered submarines belonging to the United States and the former Soviet Union have traveled deep through waters in and near the Arctic. There has been concern that one of these subs might have an accident and leak radioactive materials.

● **To the Parent**

The once-pristine Arctic faces growing pollution problems. Air pollution that reaches into the stratosphere drifts over polar regions, where it finally settles out. Ocean currents carry pollutants, as do migrating animals who introduce pesticides into the Arctic food chain. In recent years, action has been taken worldwide to protect the Arctic habitat.

How Do Wild Plants and Animals Survive in Cities?

ANSWER Cities are places where people live. Other things, however, live there too. Plants grow in bits of soil. Some animals find food and shelter in cities.

■ City wildlife

▶ Long-legged wasps nest in the eaves of buildings. They eat green caterpillars and other insects that live in cities.

▽ Dandelions are weeds that take root in the smallest bit of soil. They even grow in the cracks of sidewalks and roads.

▽ City rodents like rats and mice feed on the trash that people throw away.

▽ Daisylike plants called fleabane grow in vacant lots.

66

Swallows thrive in cities. They nest in the eaves of buildings instead of in trees.

■ Park dwellers

Many cities have parks where people are able to enjoy the sight of trees and flowers. Parks also provide ideal homes for city animals such as birds, insects, and spiders.

◀ Bulbul

▲ Orb-weaving spider

▲ Lady's-tresses orchids

● To the Parent

Many wild animals have responded to the challenge and survive quite successfully alongside humans in cities. Squirrels, raccoons, pigeons, sparrows, mice, and cockroaches are a few common examples. For adaptable animals such as these, cities provide distinct advantages, including protected nesting sites, a constant food supply, and added warmth.

Why Is It Warmer in Cities?

■ Blocking the wind

Very tall buildings can change the way wind moves through a city. At times, they can even block the wind. When this happens, warm air can be trapped in parts of the city.

■ Soaking up the heat

Cities are filled with concrete buildings and asphalt roads. These materials absorb the sun's heat. As the roads and buildings cool, they give off heat that warms the city.

ANSWER A big city can change the weather on the land where it is located. Cars and factories give off smoke and gases. This air pollution hangs over the city and traps the sun's heat. As a result, the city is often a bit warmer than the land around it.

■ Trapping warmth

When air gets warm it rises. Pollution can form a kind of umbrella over a city. Instead of escaping into the upper atmosphere, the heat from the rising air is forced back down.

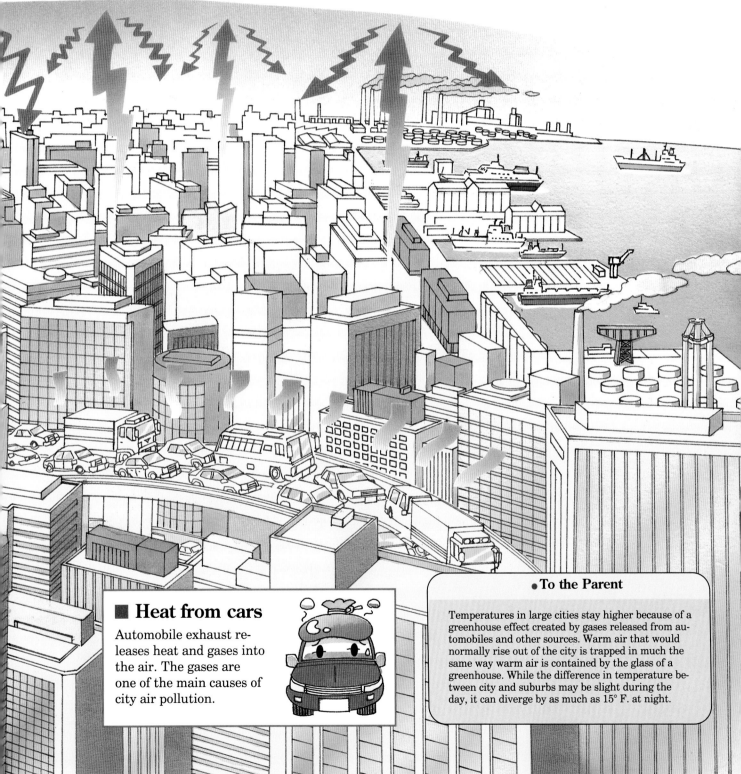

■ Heat from cars

Automobile exhaust releases heat and gases into the air. The gases are one of the main causes of city air pollution.

● To the Parent

Temperatures in large cities stay higher because of a greenhouse effect created by gases released from automobiles and other sources. Warm air that would normally rise out of the city is trapped in much the same way warm air is contained by the glass of a greenhouse. While the difference in temperature between city and suburbs may be slight during the day, it can diverge by as much as 15° F. at night.

❓ What Are People Doing to Make Cities Nicer Places to Live?

(ANSWER) Cities are crowded places. There will always be lots of people, cars, and factories. But we can do things to make them nicer, safer places to live. Improving the air we all breathe is an important first step.

■ Making air cleaner

In many countries, including the United States, there are laws that require cars to have special devices that reduce the amount of harmful gases they release. In many cities factory pollution is also carefully controlled.

▲ Without pollution controls cars really dirty the air.

▲ With pollution controls the air is cleaner and safer.

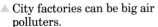

▲ City factories can be big air polluters.

▲ Special devices take most of the bad gases out of factory smoke.

Parks are an important part of city life. They are pretty islands of trees and grass surrounded by streets and buildings. In parks people can escape the busy city and enjoy nature.

■ Treelined roads

Trees planted beside the roads help make cities nicer places to live. The trees provide shade for people and homes for small animals. They also take carbon dioxide out of the air and replace it with the oxygen we need.

● **To the Parent**

Growing concern about air pollution has resulted in efforts to improve air quality in traffic-clogged cities. Automobiles are now fitted with catalytic converters, which transform certain harmful exhaust fumes into nitrogen, carbon dioxide, and water. Even so, cars present a significant pollution problem. Reducing the number of automobiles on the road through improved mass transit systems and carpooling is also part of the clean air solution. In many cities, factories have been fitted with pollution control equipment that makes the smoke and gases they release less hazardous to people.

❓ Why Is Recycling So Important?

ANSWER In our daily lives we use many materials that come from nature, such as wood, metals, and oil. These are called natural resources. It took nature a long time to make them. When we recycle a newspaper or an aluminum can, we use the materials again so we don't have to go back to nature to get more. This saves the resources that are still in the earth.

■ Saving our resources

▲ Every day people throw away mountains of garbage. Recycling reduces the amount of trash we must bury or burn.

▼ Toilet paper

▲ Cardboard boxes

Recycling

Trees

◀ Milk cartons

▲ Newspapers

▲ Magazines

Recyclable paper

Many trees are cut down to meet people's huge need for paper goods. When the paper is recycled, it can be made into new paper products. Sometimes it can be used again and again. All this recycling means fewer trees need to be cut down.

▼ **Cans and glass bottles**

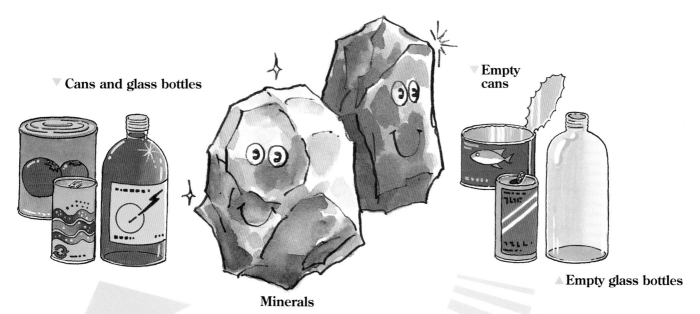

Minerals

▼ **Empty cans**

▲ **Empty glass bottles**

Recycling

Recyclable items

Glass bottles, aluminum cans, and tin-coated steel cans are all made from minerals and other raw materials that come from the earth. We can recycle these materials by melting down used bottles and cans and making them into new bottles and cans.

Plastic is made from oil, which is formed in the earth by a process that takes millions of years. Some plastic bottles can be recycled. They are cleaned and refilled or melted down and molded into other plastic products such as flower boxes.

▼ **Flower boxes**

Oil

▼ **Plastics**

Recycling

Recyclable items

● **To the Parent**

The movement to reuse and recycle materials grows in importance as landfills run out of space and the supply of certain natural resources becomes depleted. Children should be encouraged to participate in community recycling efforts.

Why Is the Earth's Ozone Layer So Important?

(ANSWER) Sunlight is very important to all living things on earth. But certain rays of the sun are harmful. These are ultraviolet rays. High in the air above our planet is a layer of ozone gas. Ozone soaks up many of the sun's ultraviolet rays and keeps them from harming us.

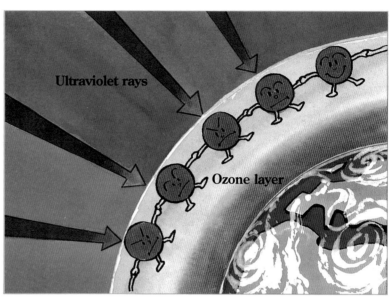

Ultraviolet rays

Ozone layer

▲ 1. When the sun's ultraviolet rays reach the ozone layer, many of them are absorbed.

■ Trouble in the ozone layer

Chlorofluorocarbons

◀ 2. Some products we use on earth release polluting chemicals called chlorofluorocarbons, or CFCs. The CFCs drift high into the air and reach the ozone layer.

▶ 3. As CFCs reach the ozone layer, the ozone breaks down. As the layer gets thinner it cannot stop as many harmful rays.

Are the Sun's Rays Harmful?

Ultraviolet rays can give people sunburn. A lot of exposure to the sun can cause skin cancer. Vegetables and simple plants like plankton are also harmed by too much of this radiation.

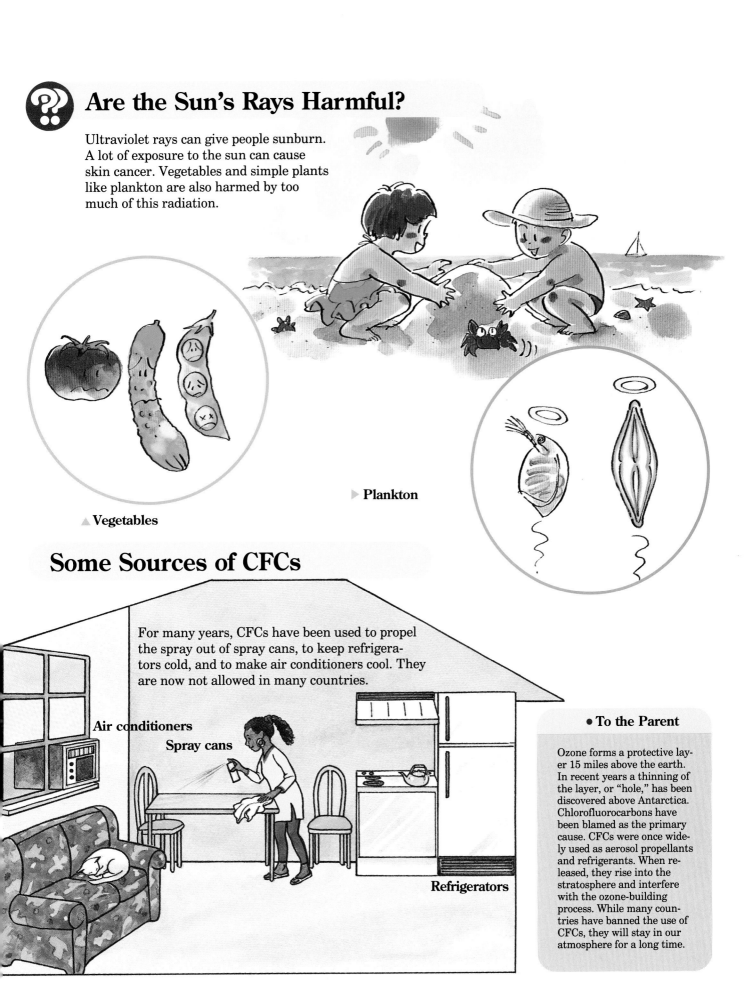

▶ **Plankton**

▲ **Vegetables**

Some Sources of CFCs

For many years, CFCs have been used to propel the spray out of spray cans, to keep refrigerators cold, and to make air conditioners cool. They are now not allowed in many countries.

Air conditioners

Spray cans

Refrigerators

? What Would Happen if the Earth Became Too Warm?

ANSWER A lot of the earth's water is frozen as ice around the North and South Poles. If temperatures on earth became too high, some of this ice would start to melt. The amount of water in the oceans would increase, and there could be floods.

■ Flooded by the ocean

■ A greenhouse effect

Gases from factories and cars form a blanket around the earth that traps warm air like the glass of a greenhouse.

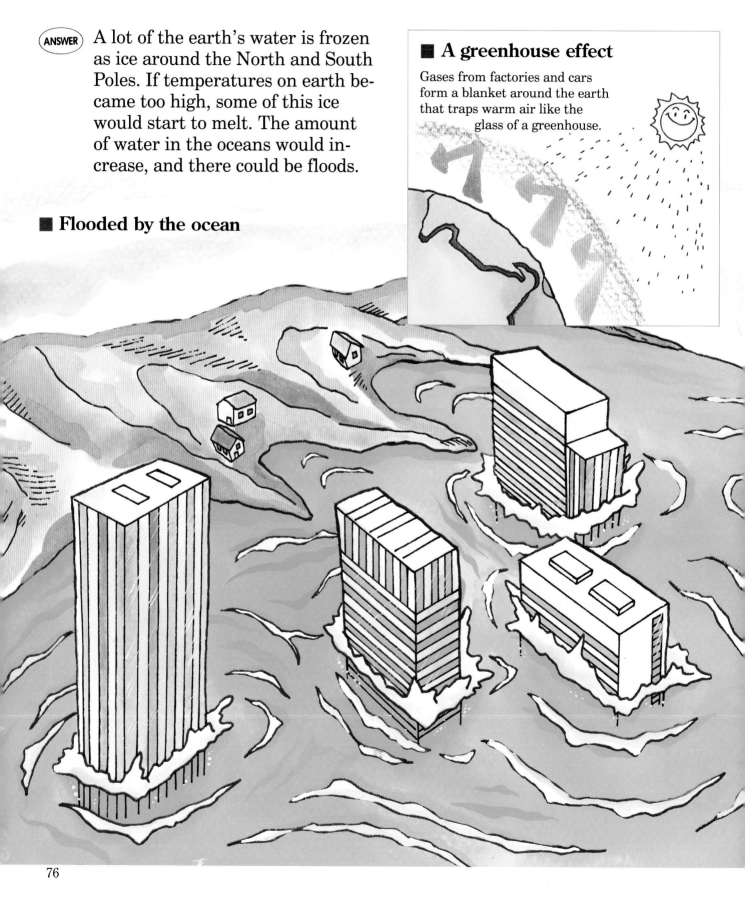

A warmer earth would change the climate around the planet. Places where farms thrive today might be too hot for crops.

The country of Bangladesh illustrates the problem of rising oceans. Most of this country is low, flat land just a bit above sea level. If the ocean level rose too much, the country would be flooded.

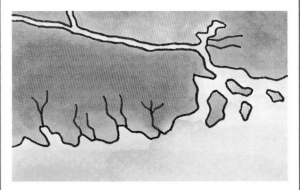

▲ **The coast of Bangladesh today**

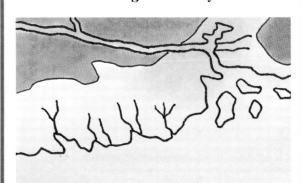

▲ **If the sea level rose 65 feet**

● **To the Parent**

The mixture of gases in the earth's atmosphere is fairly constant with one notable exception. Carbon dioxide, which accounts for only 0.05 percent of the atmosphere, is slowly increasing. This gas is released when fossil fuels such as coal or oil are burned. In the atmosphere, carbon dioxide traps heat rising from earth and prevents its escape through the atmosphere. This is the so-called greenhouse effect. Scientists are concerned that a long-term increase in carbon dioxide could alter the earth's climate. This could cause drought in farm areas, the melting of the polar icecaps, and flooding of low-lying coastal lands.

Why Do Some Animals Disappear?

(ANSWER) Earth has been home to many animals. Some, like the dinosaurs, are extinct. They are gone forever. Sometimes conditions change where animals live, and they cannot survive. People have caused some animals to become extinct.

■ Extinct animals

▶ The dodo once lived on the island of Mauritius. These harmless birds could not fly. Once people came to the island, they quickly hunted dodos to extinction.

▶ Steller's sea cow was hunted for its meat and tough hide. Only 25 years after it was discovered, it became extinct.

Schomburgk's deer was hunted for its beautiful antlers. The last deer died when people took over the area in Thailand where the deer lived.

The Tasmanian wolf was a predator on the island of Tasmania. Farmers on the island killed all the wolves so they wouldn't eat the sheep and chickens.

The extinct Réunion starling lived on the island of Réunion, 1,500 miles east of Africa. The bird's habitat was turned into farms. Starlings were killed by people and rats.

● **To the Parent**

The process of extinction has occurred naturally on our planet for hundreds of millions of years. What is new and of concern to many is the rapid rise in the rate of extinction and its effect on earth's biodiversity. A growing human population continues to change the face of the earth, often removing habitats essential to the survival of certain plants and animals. It is now estimated that thousands of species of plants and animals, many of them still undiscovered, may be lost to extinction every year.

? What Are These?

▲ Orangutan

▲ Black rhinoceros

▲ Bald eagle

▲ Hawksbill turtle

All the animals on this page belong to species that may soon be extinct if they are not protected.

▲ Giant panda

● To the Parent

Animals such as the black rhinoceros and the hawksbill turtle are poached by hunters for their valuable horns and shells. Worldwide bans on these products have been put into effect in an effort to end the poaching. Animals like the orangutan are endangered by the destruction of their forest habitats. Some countries now set aside land where animals like this may survive. Zoos have become breeding facilities for endangered species, which are sometimes reintroduced into their former wild habitats.

Growing-Up Album

Raw Materials and Recycling

In the first row are three natural resources: wood, minerals, and oil. What item in the second row is each used to make ? Through recycling, what can each resource be used to make in the third row?

A. Wood

B. Minerals

C. Oil

1. Cans, glass bottles

2. Plastics

3. Cartons, magazines

4. Flower boxes

5. Cans, glass bottles

6. Toilet paper

Answers: (A)—(3), (6); (B)—(1), (5); (C)—(2), (4).

Where Is Each Forest Found?

Forests are different in hot, mild, and cold places. Write where you would find each of these forests.

1.

2.

3.

Answers: (1) Hot places; (2) Mild places; (3) Cold places.

Caring for the Earth

Put an X in the boxes where people are harming the earth. Put a check where they are caring for it.

Throwing all garbage together instead of separating out items for recycling.

Letting your car dirty the air by not taking good care of it.

Eating all your food so none is wasted.

Taking too much food and then leaving what you cannot eat.

Forgetting to use trash cans and recycling bins.

Pouring oil and fat down the sink to get rid of them.

Putting trash in the river when you clean up your campsite.

Making sure your campfire is out before you go home.

Breaking growing branches off trees.

Answers:

People who care about the earth can do many things to help protect it:

Separate certain materials out of the trash and recycle them.

Take care of automobiles so they keep air pollution to a minimum.

Avoid littering by using trash bins and recycling containers.

Take only the food you need and eat all of it so none is wasted.

Put cooking oil and fat in the trash instead of down the sink.

Carry trash away from a campsite and dispose of it properly.

Do not do anything that harms trees and plants. Respect nature.

Who Lives in Deep Water?

The ocean is home to many animals.
Put an X next to the sea creatures that
live in deep water.

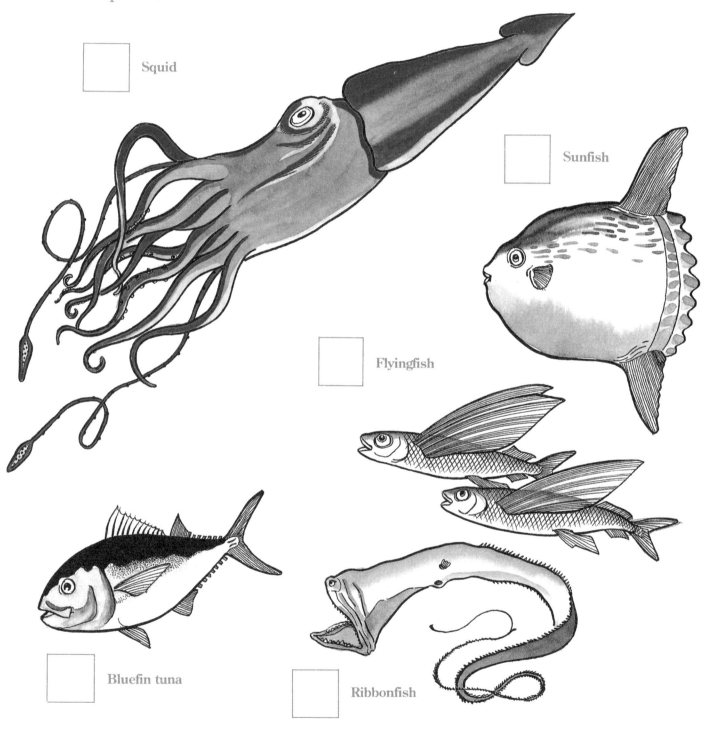

Squid

Sunfish

Flyingfish

Bluefin tuna

Ribbonfish

Answers: Squid; ribbonfish

The Arctic and the Antarctic

Although both are very cold places, the
Arctic and Antarctic are not the same.
They have differently shaped icebergs
and different animals. Which of these
is found in each place?

A. Pointed icebergs

B. Polar bears

C. Penguins

D. Flat icebergs

Answers: (A) and (B) are found in the Arctic, (C) and
(D) in the Antarctic.

A Child's First Library of Learning

Staff for
ECOLOGY

Managing Editor: Patricia Daniels
Editorial Director: Jean Burke Crawford
Research: Marike van der Veen
Production Manager: Marlene Zack
Copyeditors: Barbara Fairchild Quarmby (Senior),
    Heidi A. Fritschel
Picture Coordinator: David A. Herod
Production: Celia Beattie
Supervisor of Quality Control: James King
Assistant Supervisor of Quality Control: Miriam Newton
Library: Louise D. Forstall
Computer Composition: Deborah G. Tait (Manager),
    Monika D. Thayer, Janet Barnes Syring, Lillian Daniels

Design/Illustration: Antonio Alcalá, John Jackson,
    David Neal Wiseman
Consultant: Thomas Mullin
Photography/Illustration: 1: C. Thomas Philbrick; 8 *(top right and center)*, 9 *(center right)*, 10-11 *(top center)*, 43 *(center right)*, and 56 *(arctic fox):* art by Lili Robins; 17 *(lower left and top right)*, 38 *(bottom)*, 55 *(lower left)*, 71 *(top)*, and 75 *(bottom):* art by Linda Greigg; 46: Galen Rowell/Mountain Light; 80: *(panda)* Jessie Cohen, National Zoological Park, Smithsonian Institution, *(eagle)* U.S. Fish and Wildlife Service, photo by R. Town.
Overread: Barbara Klein

Library of Congress Cataloging-in-Publication Data
Ecology.
    p.   cm. – (A Child's First Library of Learning)
    ISBN 0-8094-9466-3. — ISBN 0-8094-9467-1 (library)
    1. Environmental sciences—Miscellanea—Juvenile literature.
    2. Environmental protection—Miscellanea—Juvenile literature. [1. Environmental sciences—Miscellanea. 2. Environmental protection—Miscellanea.] I. Time-Life Books. II. Series.
GE 115.E28 1994
363.7–dc20   93-28657
                                                     CIP
                                                     AC

TIME-LIFE for CHILDREN ©

Managing Editor: Patricia Daniels
Editorial Directors: Jean Burke Crawford, Allan Fallow,
    Karin Kinney, Sara Mark
Publishing Assistant: Marike van der Veen
Editorial Assistant: Mary M. Saxton

Original English translation by International Editorial Services Inc./C. E. Berry

First printing. Printed in U.S.A.
Published simultaneously in Canada.

Time Life Inc. is a wholly owned subsidiary of
THE TIME INC. BOOK COMPANY.

TIME LIFE is a trademark of Time Warner Inc. U.S.A.

School and library distribution by Time-Life Education,
P.O. Box 85026, Richmond, Virginia 23285-5026.
For subscription information, call 1-800-621-7026.

22977